YOU ARE
24 CARROT
GOLD

An Hachette UK Company
www.hachette.co.uk

First published in Great Britain in 2019 by Pyramid,
an imprint of Octopus Publishing Group Ltd
Carmelite House, 50 Victoria Embankment,
London EC4Y 0DZ
www.octopusbooks.co.uk

ISBN 978-0-7537-3362-2

A CIP catalogue record for this book is available from
the British Library

Printed and bound in China

10 9 8 7 6 5 4 3 2 1

Publisher: Lucy Pessell
Designer: Lisa Layton
Editor: Sarah Vaughan
Assistant Production Manager: Lucy Carter

YOU ARE 24 CARROT GOLD

words of love for someone who's worth their weight in root vegetables

To: ....

From: ....

ALOE ALOE ALOE

I YAM HERE FOR YOU
TODAY AND I WILL
BE HERE FOR YOU
TOMARROW

YOU'RE THE BEST
FIGGIN FRIEND I HAVE

I WALNUT
LEAVE YOU
BEHIND ENEMY
LIMES

ME AND YOU. I'M HAPPY WITH THIS ORANGEMENT

YOU HERB IT HERE FIRST, YOU ARE MINT

THERE'S NOTHING I'D GUAVA BE
THAN YOUR FRIEND

YOU'RE COOL BEANS

I'M HAPPIEST
WHEN I'M RIGHT
NEXT TO YUZU

I THINK YOU ARE
MARJORAMAZING

YOU ARE MY LIFE LIME

YOU FLOAT MY OAT

YOU ARE THE
MISSING PEAS OF MY HEART

I WANT TO KNOW YOU LENTIL THE
END OF THYME

IF YOU LIVE TO
BE A HUNDRED, I
WANT TO LIVE TO
BE A HUNDRED
MINUS ONE DAY,
SO I NEVER HAVE
TO LIVE WITHOUT
YUZU

WINNIE THE POOH

LETTUCE CELERYBRATE THE GOOD TIMES

YOU PUT A SPRING
ONION IN MY STEP

THERE'S SO MUSHROOM IN

MY LIFE FOR YOU

I LOVE YOU

FROM MY HEAD

TOMATOES

YOU ARE THE ONION FOR ME

YOU'RE AMAIZEING

I LEEK YOU
SO MUCH

I CAN'T REZEST YOU

YOU'RE MY
DEFINITION
OF PEARFECT

WE MAKE A
PEARFECT TEAM

I AM SUPER
GRAPEFUL FOR ALL
YOU'VE DONE FOR ME

YOU ARE THE PEA'S KNEES

YOUR
SMILE
IS LIKE
THE
SUNRICE

YOUR GRAPENESS KNOWS NO BOUNDS

WE WERE MINT TO BE FRIENDS

YOU'RE JUST TOO
GOURD TO BEETROOT

I WILL BE YOUR FRIEND
LENTIL THE END OF THYME

ENDIVE THE WORLD ENDS
TOMORROW, I WILL FACE
IT WITHOUT SORROW, FOR
MY GREATEST DREAM HAS
COME TRUE, IN THIS LIFE,
I WAS LOVED BY YUZU

RAM

YOU HAVE ALL OF MY

R . E . S . PEA . E . C . T

YOU'RE MY
RAISIN FOR LIVING

LET'S MAKE A DILL:

WE'LL BE FRIENDS FOREVER

YOU ARE THE
MISSING PEAS OF MY SOUL

I WANT TO BE
JALAPENO HEART

YOU CHIA ME UP WHEN
I'M DOWNBEET

●'●

YOU'RE

GOURDGEOUS

I NEED YOU LIKE A HEART NEEDS A BEET

RICE AND SHINE!

LETTUCE GROW OLD TOGETHER

YOU ARE
RADISHING

DID I MINTION I THINK YOU'RE GREAT!

TRUE FRIENDSHIP
NEVER DIES,

IT ONLY GETS
STRONGER WITH THYME

I'M BANANAS
ABOUT YOU

YOU HAVE REPLACED MY
NIGHTMARES WITH BEANS, MY
WORRIES WITH HAPPEANESS,
AND MY FEARS WITH LOVE

LETTUCE HAVE PEAS

ULYSSES S. GRANT

YOU'RE NOT
MY NUMBER 1

YOU'RE MY
ONION

YOU'RE UNBEETABLE

"YOU MAY SAY I'M A DREAMER...

BUT I'M NOT THE ONION"

JOHN LENNON

I'M SOY INTO YOU

THERE IS A LIGHT THAT
NEVER GOES SPROUT

THE SMITHS

DON'T WORRY,
BE A PEA

THERE IS
ONION HAPPINESS
IN THIS LIFE.
TO LOVE
AND BE LOVED

GEORGE SAND

PEAS DON'T

FIGET I LOVE YOU

THANK YUZU FOR BEING THE REASON I SMILE

COME AND AVOCUDDLE

ENDIVE I KNOW WHAT FRIENDSHIP
IS, IT'S BECAUSE OF YOU

HATERS GONNA HATE,

WE DON'T CARROT ALL

YOU'RE THE
YIN TO MY YAM

YOU MAKE MISO
VERY HAPPY

#corny

"ACASHEW SHEW SHEW, PUSH PINEAPPLE SHAKE THE TREE"

BLACK LACE

OLIVE YOU SO MUCH

I'LL CASHEW IF YOU FALL

YOU'RE ALL I AVO DREAMED OF

YOU ARE
MY SOY MATE

I WILL ALWAYS CLOVE YOU

YOU
SALSIFY
MY SOUL

YOU ARE TOATALLY AMAIZEING

#toatsamaizeballs

I WILL BE
HERE FOR YOU
COME GRAIN
OR SHINE

ALOE HA!

HIGH

CHIVE!

YOU'RE FIGGIN AMAZING

I MUSTARD MIT
I THINK YOU'RE GREAT

YOU ARE SALAD GOLD

THERE SHALLOT
OF ROOM IN MY
LIFE FOR YOU

I CHERRYSH
OUR FRIENDSHIP

YOU KNOW
YOUR ONIONS

LETTUCE
GROW
TOGETHER,
ENJOY
TOGETHER

SRI SATHYA SAI BABA

LIVIN' ON A PEAR

BON JOVI

YOU

RAISIN THE ROOF

YOU'RE MY NO GRAINER

(THIS IS GETTING OAT OF HAND)

ONCE YOU STOP CHASING
THE WRONG THINGS, THE
RIGHT ONES CASHEW

A SONG I'D SING TO YOU:

"I BAYLEAF IN MIRACLES, SINCE YUZU CAME ALONG"

HOT CHOCOLATE

I AM YOUR CHIA LEADER

"I SAY A LITTLE PEAR FOR YOU"

DIONNE WARWICK

NIGHT, NIGHT,

SWEDE DREAMS

THAT
SHALLOT!

For those of you who haven't herb enough, and haven't herb-it-all-bivore, this series has all the chiaing things you've ever wanted to say in vegan-friendly puns* covered.

Find the pearfect gift for any occasion:

DON'T GIVE A FIG
words of wisdom for when
life gives you lemons

YOU ARE MY RAISIN FOR LIVING
words for someone who's
just the pea's knees

AVOCUDDLE
comfort words for when you're
feeling downbeet

I AM GRAPEFUL
all the good thymes I want to
thank you for

WHATAMELON
comforting pick-you-ups
for epic fails

*Or plant-based puns if, like us, you are no longer sure if avocados are vegan. Or friendly.

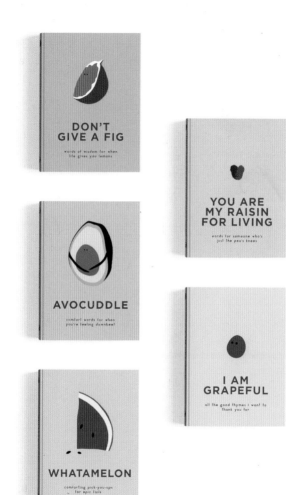

Acknowledgements and Apologies

With thanks to Andrew, Anna, Steph and Matt for their contributions, and special thanks to Joe as his contributions were really quite good.

We regret not being able to say anything nice with cavolo nero, kohl rabi, sorrel and fenugreek. We hold anyone who can in the highest regard.

"patience is bitter but its fruit is sweet"
Aristotle